ADAPTATION FOR SURVIVAL

EARS

WRITTEN BY STEPHEN SAVAGE

Thomson Learning
New York

ADAPTATION FOR SURVIVAL

Books in the series

• EARS • EYES • HANDS AND FEET
• MOUTHS • NOSES • SKIN

Front cover: A pair of African elephants, children whispering,
a hippo's ears.

Back cover: Children whispering.

Title page: House mice eating spilled wheat.

First published in the United States in 1995 by
Thomson Learning
115 Fifth Avenue
New York, NY 10003

Published simultaneously in Great Britain by Wayland (Publishers) Limited

U.S. version copyright © 1995 Thomson Learning

U.K. version copyright © 1995 Wayland (Publishers) Limited

Library of Congress Cataloging-in-Publication
Savage, Stephen, 1965–
    Ears / written by Stephen Savage.
        p.   cm.—(Adaptation for survival)
    Includes bibliographical references and index.
    ISBN 1-56847-350-8
        1. Hearing—Juvenile literature. 2. Ear—Juvenile literature.
    [1. Hearing. 2. Ear.] I. Title. II. Series: Savage, Stephen, 1965–
    Adaptation for survival.
    QP462.2.S28   1995
    591.1'825—dc20   94-23962

Printed in Italy

Contents

Human Ears

Humans have very good hearing. All the sounds that we hear travel through the air as vibrations. Our external, visible ears collect sound from all around us, which is then funneled into the inner ear. The sound passes from the inner ear to the brain, where it is identified. Our ears are in a good position for recognizing the direction that the sound comes from.

▲ *Human ears are similar to those of most mammals. The visible part of the ear (external ear) is used to collect sounds from around us.*

▼ *This is a diagram of the human ear, showing the main features. See page 31 for more details of how we hear.*

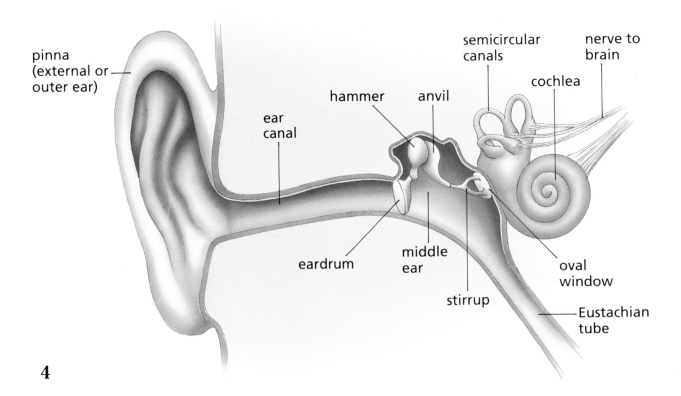

4

Our ears pick up sound almost every moment of the day: traffic, voices, machinery, a barking dog. Our ears can pick out the one sound that we want to hear. For example, we may have little problem hearing a friend talking to us in a crowded street.

Animals have ears that are suited to their way of life. Some have ears that are similar to human ears, while others have ears that are very different. Some animals have hearing better than ours, but other animals have very poor hearing or none at all.

Like many animals, we use sight and hearing together. We can hear as well as see traffic approaching.
The sound of a car horn, a dog barking, or a shout, may cause us to look in that direction.

5

Listening for Danger

An animal's hearing often acts as an early warning system. Many small mammals are hunted and eaten by predators. These small mammals have large external ears that are good for collecting sound. Mice have poor eyesight, but they have excellent hearing.

Mice are more active at night and, as they forage for food, their large ears help them to listen for any sound that may mean danger.

6

Hares and rabbits also have large ears and good hearing. Hares do not live underground, so they have to rely on hearing danger when it is a long way off. A rabbit's hearing is not as good as that of a hare is, but rabbits are never far from the safety of their burrows.

Some large mammals also need good hearing to warn them of danger. Antelope are in danger of attack by lions and cheetahs. Their sensitive hearing warns them of danger, giving them time to run to safety.

An aardvark has long sensitive ears that pick up sound as a warning of danger. Aardvarks escape from danger by burrowing.

A deer can quickly move its ears in the direction of the slightest sound. Once the direction of the sound has been found, the deer uses its excellent eyesight to see if there is any danger.

Listening for Food

Most animals that catch and eat other animals for food have large ears to help them find their prey. These predators often use both sight and hearing together. They may hear the movement of their prey first and then use sight in the final attack. Foxes, wolves, and even the domestic cat use hearing and sight in this way.

For hunting in thick vegetation, a good sense of hearing is more useful than sight to a tiger.

8

◀ Lions live and hunt in a group. Markings on the back of a lioness's ears allow other members of the group to see her, as they hunt their prey together.

▼ Foxes have very good hearing that will alert them to the sound of potential danger.

Predators have ears that can be turned toward the slightest sound. We cannot move our ears in this way; instead, we have to move our heads. Like humans, predators can easily tell the direction a sound comes from. If the sound comes from the right, it will reach the right ear a split second before it reaches the left one.

Bears eat other animals and plants. They do not need large ears for finding food, and their large size means they have little to fear from attack.

Hunting at Night

Our hearing is quite good at night because there is less traffic and other noise disturbance to distract us. Some animals choose to hunt at night, and their hearing is far better than our own.

Some scientists think that the owl's face-disk may have the same use as our external ears. The disk may collect sound for the ears, which are underneath the edge of the disk.

Owls are one of the most successful of the night hunters. They can even hear the rustling sound of a mouse foraging for food. One ear may be higher or larger than the other, which helps it pinpoint the exact position of its prey.

The owl has soft feathers so that it can fly silently and not be heard by its intended meal. Its hearing is so sensitive that it can catch prey in complete darkness.

10

Leopards often hunt their prey at night. They hunt alone and will stalk and catch small mammals and birds.

Leopards and many other big cats hunt mainly at night. They find their prey by using their hearing and night vision. Galagos also have very sensitive hearing and can hear the movement of their insect prey as they hunt high up in the trees.

This galago's large ears are good for hearing insects. It can grab a flying insect from the air with its hands! The galago also has large eyes to help it find its way around in the branches.

11

Seeing with Sound

A few animals, including bats, can actually "see" by using sound. If you shout while walking through a tunnel, you will hear your shout come back as an echo. The shrew, a small mammal, finds its way around its tunnels by making noises and listening for the echo.

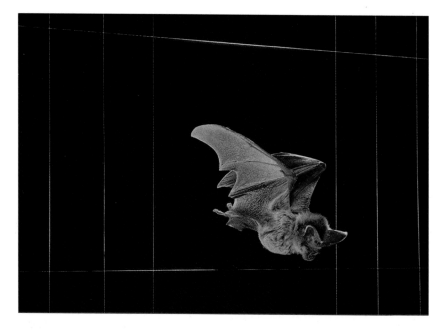

Bats have very large ears. They make noises as they fly in the night sky and listen for the echo from nearby objects. This is called echolocation and is similar to radar. This bat is making noises and listening to the echo made by the wires so that it doesn't fly into them.

Bats make very high-pitched sounds that we cannot hear. When these sounds hit a nearby object, they return to the bat as an echo. A bat's hearing is much better than a human's—it can listen to the echo and make sure that it doesn't fly into a tree or other object. Bats can also use echoes to help them catch flying insects.

12

Some animals like bats and dolphins have a natural built-in system for avoiding collision, but people have to use special machinery to help ships and planes avoid collision. These air traffic controllers are using a system called radar to locate planes approaching the airport and help them land safely.

Dolphins also make sounds to help them catch fish and to find their way around when the sea is murky. Sperm whales make sounds to find food in the darkest depths of the ocean.

Dolphins do not have external ears. They use their jaws and teeth to collect sound vibrations from the surrounding water. The sound vibrations pass through the jaw and into the inner ear.

Hearing Underwater

Except for the sound of waves crashing on the seashore, the sea was once thought to be a silent place. We now know that the sea is filled with the sounds of courting fish, feeding animals, and singing whales.

Most fish have an air-filled swim bladder that prevents them from sinking. In some fish, the inner ears are connected to the swim bladder, which collects sound vibrations and passes them on to the ear.

Our external ears are adapted for hearing in air. Sound travels much better underwater than it does in air, so we can hear some muffled sounds underwater. As sound travels so well in water, it is not surprising that many sea creatures have good hearing and communicate using sound.

Fish have good hearing, but they do not need external ears. Sound vibrations pass through the fish's body and are then heard by the inner ears. Fish make a wide range of clicks, grunts, and chirping sounds to attract a mate or warn off a rival. Clams and other shellfish make sounds by opening and closing their shells.

Lobsters sometimes make sounds by rubbing the base of their large antennae against their shells. The lobster's ears are two special short antennae that pick up sound vibrations.

▲ *Sharks have very good hearing and are often attracted by sound. They can hear sounds some distance away. Sharks are particularly good at hearing the sounds made by injured fish.*

15

Keeping Cool, Keeping Warm

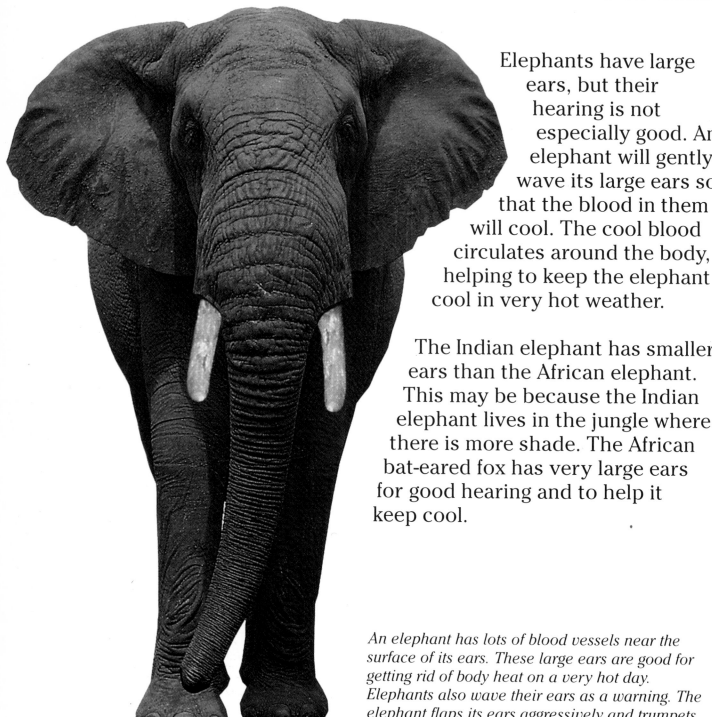

Elephants have large ears, but their hearing is not especially good. An elephant will gently wave its large ears so that the blood in them will cool. The cool blood circulates around the body, helping to keep the elephant cool in very hot weather.

The Indian elephant has smaller ears than the African elephant. This may be because the Indian elephant lives in the jungle where there is more shade. The African bat-eared fox has very large ears for good hearing and to help it keep cool.

An elephant has lots of blood vessels near the surface of its ears. These large ears are good for getting rid of body heat on a very hot day. Elephants also wave their ears as a warning. The elephant flaps its ears aggressively and trumpets through its trunk to warn off a dangerous animal.

16

Fennec foxes use their large ears for hearing danger and also for keeping cool in the hot deserts where they live in North Africa and the Arabian peninsula.

Very few mammals live in the cold Arctic. Those that do are protected by a thick layer of fur and fat. The polar bear and Arctic fox live in the cold, harsh Arctic environment. These animals have short, rounded ears that are covered in fur. Unlike the ears of the elephant and bat-eared fox, these ears are adapted to help keep the animal warm.

The Arctic fox has small, rounded ears that are covered in fur. These small ears help keep the animal from losing heat during the freezing winter.

Where Are My Ears?

An animal's ears are not always visible. In fact, the ears of some animals are not even on their heads. Crickets have their ears inside their front legs. The ear has a simple eardrum covering a small hole. Crickets can tell the direction of a sound by waving these legs around in the air.

Most grasshoppers have their ears on the sides of their bodies or on their legs. One of the many uses of an earwig's tail pincers may be to collect sound vibrations.

▲ *It is mainly noisy insects, like crickets and grasshoppers, that have hearing. Many insects are deaf. This East African grasshopper is showing its "ears," which are normally hidden by its wings.*

Spiders like this tarantula have special hairs on their legs for sensing the movement of their insect prey. Some insects hear using special hairs, while others have special antennae. Some moths can hear the sounds made by bats and fly to avoid them. ▶

Although fish have ears inside their heads, they also have another way of hearing. If you look closely at a fish, you will see a line of small holes on its body, running from the head to the tail. Sound vibrations in the water are "heard" through these holes. A blind cave fish can find its way around in the darkness using this sense.

The holes along the side of this goldfish are called the lateral line. This extra hearing sense can warn the fish of danger or help a shoal of fish to swim together.

Poor Hearing

Many small animals have very poor hearing. Like the cricket, some animals can only hear other members of their own species or the approach of danger. Snakes have no external ears or eardrums. They can, however, sense low-frequency sounds such as approaching footsteps. Strangely enough, a rattlesnake cannot hear its own rattle!

This male mosquito uses its feathery antennae to pick up the sound vibrations made by a female mosquito's wings. Many insects can "hear" very simple sounds by using antennae or special hairs.

The male coqui frog from Puerto Rico produces a two syllable call, "Ko-Kee." The first part of the call, "Ko," is only heard by males and is a warning call. The second part of the call, "Kee," is only heard by females and is used to attract a mate.

The spadefoot toad lives in the desert, far away from water. It spends much of the time buried under the sand. The spadefoot toad will become active and return to the surface again when it hears the pitter-patter of rain.

▲ *Frogs are very vocal and make a variety of sounds to attract a mate or warn off a rival. Many frogs have throat sacs that amplify their calls, such as this common African toad. Its vocal sac remains fully inflated during the breeding period.*

◄ *Although frogs do not have external ears, they do have large, visible eardrums. The ears of this American bullfrog are bigger than its eyes.*

21

Here I Am!

Many animals rely on sound and hearing to communicate with one another. This is especially important for animals that live in forests or woodlands. In such places, it is difficult for these animals to keep in contact with other members of their group.

Some birds, like this European song thrush, advertise their presence through song. The song is used to attract a mate and defend the bird's territory.

Mangabey monkeys live high up in the branches of the African rain forest. Visual signals are not much use, so they communicate with each other using a variety of grunts and barks. The males of each group make a "whoop-gobble" call to warn other groups that they are nearby.

It is often murky underwater and difficult to see any great distance. Whales and dolphins keep in contact with other members of their group using sound. Some types of whale, like the male humpback whale, sing a complex song to attract a mate. Some parts of the song can be heard up to fifty miles away.

Groups of howler monkeys call in the early morning and when on the move during the day. This keeps accidental meetings and clashes between rival howler monkey groups to a minimum. These monkeys are the noisiest land mammals.

Some types of whale, like this killer whale, perform aerial acrobatics. The whale leaps out of the water, twists its body in the air, and crashes back down into water. This loud noise may be heard by other whales some distance away.

Private Talk

When we want to talk to a friend without anyone else hearing, we talk in a whisper. Some animals communicate using sounds that our ears are not sensitive enough to hear. Elephants produce very deep (low-frequency) sounds to talk to other members of the herd, who are often scattered over a wide area.

▲ *The chicks of some ground-nesting birds can "talk" to each other while still inside their eggs. This is thought to help the chicks to hatch at the same time and follow their mother soon after hatching.*

An elephant can warn the rest of the herd of danger by making low, rumbling sounds. Although humans cannot hear them, these sounds can be heard by other elephants several miles away. ▶

24

Mice and rats talk to each other in high-pitched squeaks. This is a good way for communicating in tunnels under the ground. Unlike low-frequency sounds that travel great distances, high-pitched sounds are quickly absorbed by the surrounding earth. This means that the sound will travel around the tunnels but will not be heard above the ground by predators.

Whales talk to each other in a variety of groans, grunts, and rumbles. Sound travels much farther at certain depths in the sea. Some whales dive down to these depths to call other whales that are a long way off.

Some squeaks made by mice are too high-pitched for humans to hear, but they are heard by other mice. Because mice have sensitive hearing, high-pitched sounds can be used as a humane way of chasing away rodent pests.

25

Mother and Young

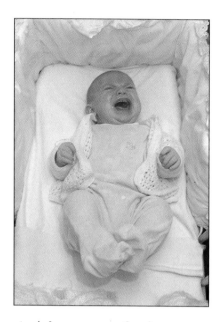

Like humans, most animals can hear before they are born. As with all mammals, a human baby develops inside its mother's body. The first thing a baby hears is its mother's heartbeat. Later, it is able to hear muffled sounds from outside its mother's body.

▲ *A human mother's soothing voice will calm her baby. Although the baby cannot yet understand words, it responds to the sound and tone of its mother's voice.*

A mother duck will often call her reluctant chicks into the water for their first swim. She will also give a warning call if danger is nearby. ▶

26

After they are born, baby animals learn about the world around them through their ears and eyes. Sound is an important way for young animals to communicate with their mothers. A human baby will cry when it wants to be fed. Birds call to their parents when they are hungry. Newly hatched crocodiles will call to their mother, so that she will dig them out of the mound nest that protected them as eggs.

Some animal mothers make special sounds so that the young animals will follow them. A seal pup does not know it can swim until it follows its mother into the sea.

A seal mother knows the sound of her own pup. When returning from a swim, she can recognize its call from all the others. This is an Australian sealion greeting her pup.

What Did You Say?

Animals with the most complex hearing make the widest variety of sound for communication. "Animal language" can range from simple grunts and squeaks to the detailed sounds that are made by some whales. Humans have the most complex language. We use thousands of different words, which make up sentences.

Language is an important part of our lives. It can take the form of a simple greeting or it can be used to pass on complicated information to others. Our language contains thousands of words that we can make into meaningful sentences.

28

Animals that live in groups have the most need for language. Many calls are of a social nature and help to strengthen bonds among group members. Many animals have calls that warn of danger. When a dwarf mongoose gives the alarm call, the rest of the pack scatters for cover.

Killer whales live in family groups and communicate using a variety of sounds. Each killer whale group has its own unique calls. These whales also "squeak" with an accent, so each individual whale has a recognizable voice.

▲ *Chimpanzees live in groups. They communicate with each other using a variety of soft grunts, hoots, and shrieks. Scientists have identified thirteen different types of sound that chimpanzees use to communicate.*

Beluga whales have been called "the canaries of the sea." These whales communicate using a wide range of calls including moos, chirps, whistles, and clangs. As with many other animals, we have yet to unravel the mystery of the beluga's calls. ▶

Glossary

Amplify To make louder.

Antennae Feelers on the head of an insect, lobster, or similar animal.

Complex Complicated.

Communicate To pass information from one animal (or person) to another.

Courtship Finding or attracting a mate.

Foraging Searching for food.

Frequency The number of times a sound vibrates in a second. The higher the frequency, the higher the sound.

Predator An animal that kills other animals for food.

Swim bladder An air-filled organ that most fish have, which stops them from sinking.

Unravel To discover the meaning of something.

Further Reading

Bennett, Paul. *Escaping from Enemies.* Nature's Secrets. New York: Thomson Learning, 1995.

Darling, David. *Sounds Interesting: The Science of Acoustics.* Experiment! New York: Dillon Press, 1991.

Parker, Steve. *The Ear and Hearing.* The Human Body. Revised edition. New York: Franklin Watts, 1989.

Further Notes

Humans have five senses, each of which contributes to our awareness of our environment, therefore helping us to survive. All animals view the world through a combination of senses. Their senses collect information that is relevant to their survival, so many animals perceive the world differently from the way humans do.

30

Parts of the human ear

Pinna – The name for the external ear that collects sounds that are funneled into the inner ear.

Eardrum – The flap of skin between the outer and middle ear, held tight like the skin of a drum.

Ear bones – Three bones in the middle ear - the malleus, incus, and stapes. They are also known as the hammer, anvil, and stirrup. These bones amplify the sound and pass it on into the inner ear.

Hammer – The first of the middle ear bones. The hammer is connected to the eardrum.

Anvil – The second of the three bones in the middle ear.

Stirrup – The third of the three bones in the middle ear.

Cochlea – The coiled inner ear, which is filled with fluid. Sound vibrations in the inner ear pass to special nerves.

Nerve – Fiber that connects the brain spinal cord with other parts of the body. A nerve carries sound signals from the inner ear to the brain, where they are interpreted.

Eustachian tube – Tube that connects the middle ear to the back of the nose. The tube opens to keep air pressure in the middle ear the same as the air pressure outside the ear.

Semicircular canals – Structures in the inner ear that are concerned with balance. They have nothing to do with hearing.

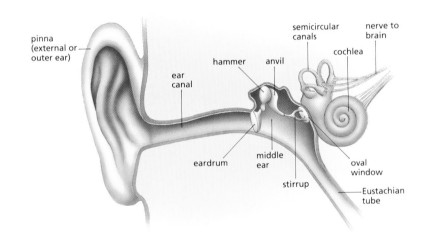

How we hear
The human ear has three parts – the pinna, or outer ear, the middle ear, and the inner ear. Sound vibrations travel through the air and are collected by the pinna (outer ear). The sound vibrations are funneled into the inner ear where they vibrate the eardrum. The vibrations are passed to three special bones (hammer, anvil, and stirrup) in the middle ear, where they are amplified. The vibrations pass into the inner ear (the cochlea) and are sent through special nerves to the brain, where the sound is identified.

Balance
The semicircular canals in the inner ear help you to balance by telling your brain about your position in space. For example, they help us to bend over to pick up an object without losing our balance and falling. Most mammals have a similar organ connected to their ears. Other animals, such as bees, have special hairs on their backs that tell them if they are the right way up or upside-down.

31

Index

32